SCHOLASTIC
News
Nonfiction Readers

W9-BLU-179

Let's Vote on It!

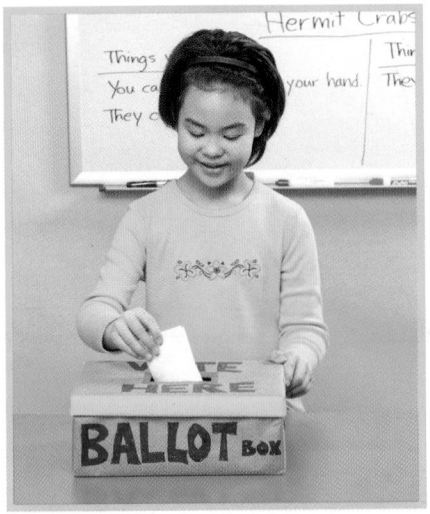

By Janice Behrens

Children's Press®
An Imprint of Scholastic Inc.
New York Toronto London Auckland Sydney
Mexico City New Delhi Hong Kong
Danbury, Connecticut

These content vocabulary word builders are for grades 1–2.

Subject Consultant: Eli J. Lesser, MA, Director of Education, National Constitution Center, Philadelphia, Pennsylvania

Reading Consultant: Cecilia Minden-Cupp, PhD, Early Literacy Consultant and Author, Chapel Hill, North Carolina

Photographs © 2010: iStockphoto: 5 inset (Steve Goodwin), 5 inset (Eric Isselee); All other photographs ©Ken Karp.

Art Direction, Production, and Digital Imaging: Scholastic Classroom Magazines

Library of Congress Cataloging-in-Publication Data

Behrens, Janice, 1972-
Let's vote on it! / Janice Behrens.
p. cm. – (Scholastic news nonfiction readers)
Includes bibliographical references and index.
ISBN 13: 978-0-531-21346-9 (lib. bdg.) 978-0-531-21445-9 (pbk.)
ISBN 10: 0-531-21346-3 (lib. bdg.) 0-531-21445-1 (pbk.)
1. Voting–United States–Juvenile literature. 2. Elections–United States–Juvenile literature. I. Title. II. Series.
JK1978.B45 2009 324.60973–dc22 2009006373

No part of this publication may be reproduced in whole or in part, or stored in a retrieval system, or transmitted in any form or by any means, electronic, mechanical, photocopying, recording, or otherwise, without written permission of the publisher. For information regarding permission, write to Scholastic Inc., 557 Broadway, New York, NY 10012.

©2010 Scholastic Inc.
All rights reserved. Published in 2010 by Children's Press, an imprint of Scholastic Inc.
Published simultaneously in Canada. Printed in the United States of America.
SCHOLASTIC, CHILDREN'S PRESS, and associated logos are trademarks and/or registered trademarks of Scholastic Inc.
1 2 3 4 5 6 7 8 9 10 R 18 17 16 15 14 13 12 11 10 09

CONTENTS

Vote for a Class Pet 4–7

Time to Choose 8–11

Which Pet Wins? 12–15

Let's Keep Voting 16–19

My Mom Votes! 20–21

Your New Words 22–23

Index 24

Find Out More 24

Meet the Author 24

Vote for a Class Pet

We are getting a class pet!

We can get a goldfish or a hermit crab. How can we choose?

We will take a **vote**!

Which pet should we choose?

First, we read books about goldfish. We read about hermit crabs, too.

We talk about what we like and do not like about each pet. That helps us choose which pet we want.

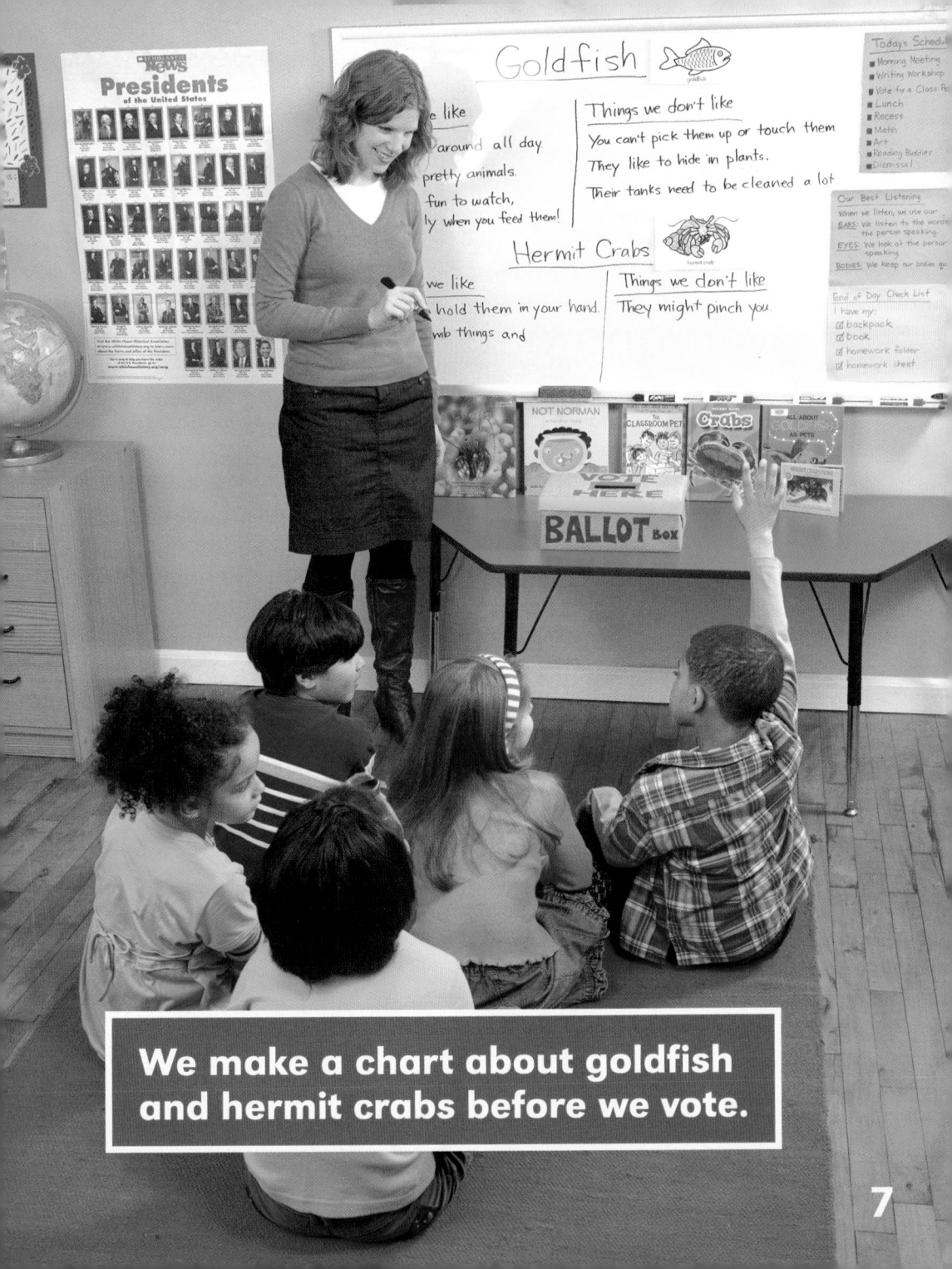

We make a chart about goldfish and hermit crabs before we vote.

Time to Choose

Now we are ready to vote! Everyone gets a **ballot**. A ballot shows your choices when you vote.

We each color our choice on the ballot. Which pet would you choose?

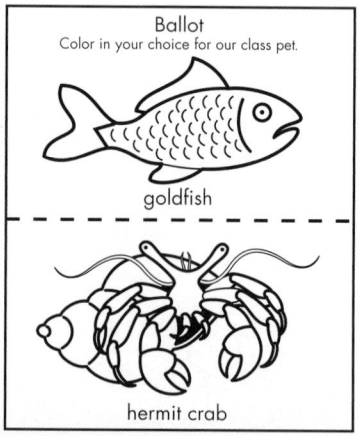

ballot

Crayola

Next, we fold our ballots. Then, we put them in a **ballot box**.

Our teacher says we do not have to tell anyone how we vote.

We take turns putting our ballots in the box.

Which Pet Wins?

Finally our teacher counts the votes. She makes a **tally** to keep count.

The pet with the most votes will win! Which pet do you think will be the winner?

It's time to count the votes!

The goldfish wins! More kids voted for the goldfish.

Some of us voted for the hermit crab. That's OK! We will get to vote again. Soon we will vote for a name for the goldfish.

Goldfish
Hermit Crab
Todays Schedule
Morning Meeting
Writing Workshop
Vote for a Class Pet!
Lunch
Recess
Math
Art
ALL ABOUT
AS PETS
BOX

Let's Keep Voting

Voting is a fair way for a **group** to make a choice. You can even vote with your friends!

Which game would you vote for, kickball or jump rope?

Who wants to play kickball at recess? Who wants to jump rope?

Adults vote, too. In the United States, adults vote to choose our **leaders**.

When you grow up, you can vote to **elect**, or choose, our leaders. Until then, you can vote for kickball!

SCHOLASTIC News
Presidents
of the United States
A friend is:
Thoughtful
Trustworthy
A good listener

MY MOM VOTES!

Adults vote for our leaders. My mom lets me go with her when she votes.

1. We vote at a polling place. A polling place can be a school, library, or other place in your neighborhood.

2. We wait in line for our turn.

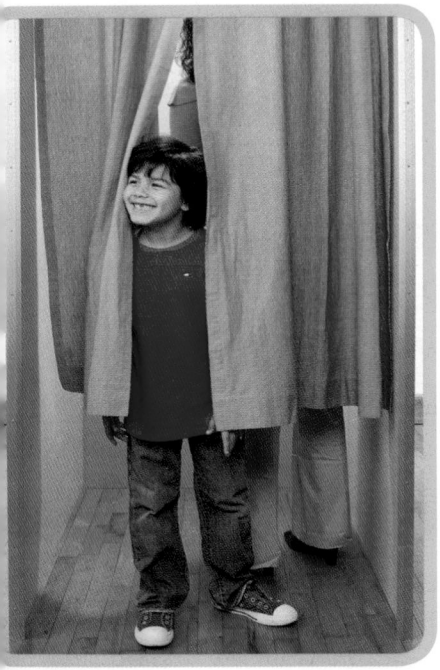

3. Mom goes into a oting booth. Inside, he pulls a lever to ote. She chooses the eople she thinks will o the best job.

4. I know who my mom voted for. But I won't tell! Her vote is a secret.

YOUR NEW WORDS

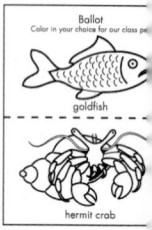

ballot (**bal**-uht) a piece of paper that gives the choices in a secret vote

ballot box (**bal**-uht boks) a box with a slit on top to put votes in

elect (i-**lekt**) to choose by voting

group (groop) a number of people who work together or share something

aders (**lee**-durz) people in charge who make decisions, like Presidents of the United States

ılly (**tal**-ee) a count or a score

ote (voht) a way of making a decision where everyone offers a choice and the most popular choice wins

INDEX

adults, 18, 20

ballot box, 10
ballots, 8, 10
books, 6

choices, 8, 16
class pet, 4, 6, 8, 12, 14
counting, 12

electing, 18

goldfish, 4, 6, 8, 14

hermit crabs, 4, 6, 8, 14

jump rope, 16

kickball, 16, 18

leaders, 18, 20
lever, 21

polling place, 20

reading, 6

talking, 6
tally, 12
teacher, 10, 12

voting booth, 21

FIND OUT MORE

Book:
Christelow, Eileen. *Vote!* New York: Clarion Books, 2008.

Website:
The Democracy Project: PBS Kids
http://pbskids.org/democracy/vote

MEET THE AUTHOR

Janice Behrens is a writer and Scholastic editor. She lives in Brooklyn, New York, with her family.